THE REALLY USEFUL
Garden Bird
HANDBOOK

Mark Ward

FIRST STONE

Published by
First Stone
A Division of Corpus Publishing Limited
PO Box 8, Lydney, Gloucestershire GL15 6YD

Cover design: Sarah Flitcroft

ISBN 1 904439 48 9

Manufactured in Singapore

10 9 8 7 6 5 4 3 2 1

Photography: Dave and Brian Bevan

Additional photographs: Graham Catley and Gordon Langsbury

The publishers would like to thanks Gardman Limited for their help in
providing feeders and nest-boxes for photographic purposes.

CONTENTS

WHY ATTRACT GARDEN BIRDS?

All the effort you put into making your garden a haven for birds will be repaid many times over by the hours of entertainment they provide. And you can rest in the knowledge that you are doing something very positive to help our threatened wild birds.

They need as much help as possible from humans. The countryside continues to contract as a result of development. There are fewer nesting and feeding areas for wild birds – and many modern farming methods are not wildlife friendly.

- **Thousands of miles of hedgerow have been ripped out.**
- **Super-efficient pesticides and herbicides have removed natural food sources in the form of insects and wildflower seeds.**
- **Vast tracts of countryside have been concreted over for development.**
- **Modern building design often excludes birds that once nested under the rafters and in holes in the exterior.**

Unsurprisingly, many once-common bird species have suffered catastrophic falls in population. Even the humble House Sparrow and Starling – familiar birds to everyone

The House Sparrow, once a common sight in our gardens, is now under threat.

You do not need a large garden to attract a variety of birds.

– are nowhere near as common as they used to be. The House Sparrow declined by 65 per cent between 1970 and 2001 in the UK.

At the same time, gardens have become increasingly vital refuges for wildlife. The total space of all the gardens in Britain amounts to more than one million acres, and your garden can become another vital link in the growing chain of 'artificial countryside'.

A colourful crowd

Visiting wild birds provide a constant display of colour in your garden throughout the year.

Many people are surprised at just how attractive and colourful British birds are. Ranging from the rainbow colours of the male Chaffinch, to the beautiful glossy blue, green and purple sheen seen in a Starling's feathers on a sunny day, each of our garden birds is a joy to behold.

They also provide a wonderful natural soundtrack with their songs and calls. In spring, they produce a concert performance each morning during the 'dawn chorus'. You can be serenaded by Song Thrushes in the mornings and evenings, and during summer evenings you can relax to the soft chirping calls of House Martins soaring in the sky.

Attracting birds into the garden will provide you with an unbeatable insight into the fascinating lives of

WHY ATTRACT GARDEN BIRDS?

You may be lucky enough to see birds such as this Song Thrush raising their young.

birds on a daily basis. Many garden birds allow close-up views that would be almost impossible to find in the countryside, where birds are generally much less approachable. Garden birds can become very tame and confiding – such as the Robin that perches on your spade while you are digging the garden.

You can follow the ups and downs of the birds that visit your garden, and you will get to know individual birds and their families. Some will return to your garden regularly or become residents for their lifetime. You can watch the best soap opera ever as you witness the neighbourly disputes of Robins or the comical flock of squabbling Starlings at the bird table, and you will be endlessly entertained, watching how different species – and different individuals – behave.

What better stress-reliever is there than to settle back in your favourite armchair and observe the antics of the garden birds through the window or from your conservatory?

Breeding season

Birds will come to feed, drink and bathe throughout the year, but the breeding season brings the added excitement and thrill of seeing your garden birds raise their young.

You can follow the trials and tribulations of the birds that choose to nest in, or near to, your garden, celebrate as they successfully rear their young, and watch the fledglings depart and make their own way in the world. There isn't always a happy ending – but many species have a second or third brood to help compensate for any disasters that may befall them.

There is always something new to learn about garden birds. As you watch them closely, you will find that you want to discover the reasons for certain types of behaviour.

Garden birds will continually surprise and delight. There is the added challenge of trying new food or introducing nest-boxes – and seeing if your innovations pay off. Without a doubt, 'bird gardening' is every bit as interesting, relaxing, stimulating and rewarding as conventional gardening.

Watching the private lives of garden birds is better than any soap opera!

FEEDING BIRDS

The single, most effective measure you can take to attract wild birds is to provide them with food. There is a huge range of 'supplementary' food that will be suitable for birds in the garden. Much is inexpensive, and birds are certainly not too proud to feast on leftovers from our meal tables, or on any unwanted food we may have, so it does not have to be a big expense.

You can provide as much or as little food as you like – anything will be gratefully received. The more types you provide, the more species you will attract. The list of suitable foods later in this chapter will help you decide what to offer.

Different species not only have different food preferences, they also feed in different ways. For example, Dunnocks and Blackbirds prefer to forage on the ground, while tits hang from branches. This chapter also outlines the different ways in which you can serve food for garden birds.

Winter shortages

When natural food is scarce, particularly when snow covers the ground, the food put out in gardens will save the lives of many birds. Having access to a well-stocked garden, on a daily basis, can mean the difference between life and death for small birds during winter.

Knowing that food is constantly available in one place ensures that birds do not need to use their valuable supplies of energy (in the form of the fat reserves they have built up) in seeking or hunting for food elsewhere.

All-year benefits

Feeding garden birds was once considered to be a winter-only

Winter is a tough time for birds.

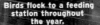

Birds flock to a feeding station throughout the year.

necessity, and experts used to recommend that you confined feeding to that season. However, new research has shown that feeding throughout the year has many benefits for birds:

• Some species suffer losses during spring because natural foods, such as nuts, seeds, berries and insects, are not common.
• British spring weather is unpredictable, and spells of rain and cold weather, which hamper natural feeding, are common.

• Adults of species such as Goldfinches and Greenfinches often struggle to find enough food for themselves early in the breeding season, and may starve to death.

If you continue providing supplementary food throughout the spring, the well-fed adult birds can then concentrate on finding the natural foods, such as insects, which they prefer to feed to their young.

It may seem as if there is plenty of natural food available during the long, hot days of summer, but the

FEEDING BIRDS

breeding season is a tough time for birds.

They have to make sure they get into, and stay in, peak condition for the rigours of raising a family. A good diet means healthy birds, and these are the ones that are most likely to both attract a mate and raise their young successfully.

You will soon see if the birds are still dependent on the food you put out during the summer and whether their visits decrease. You can therefore react accordingly, reducing the amount of food you put out if necessary.

Providing food throughout the year also ensures that birds become a permanent, year-round fixture in the garden. Suddenly stopping the supply of food can take the birds by surprise and they may head elsewhere.

I am often asked when you should feed garden birds. Personally, I believe in feeding throughout the year, but cutting down the amount during summer and autumn when natural food is in relative abundance.

How often?

The most important times for feeding birds – especially during winter – are first thing in the morning and last thing in the afternoon, so make sure there is always food available at these times.

Birds need to prepare themselves for the long winter nights by building up their energy levels and fat reserves to 'burn' overnight as fuel to maintain their body temperature. They must ensure they have eaten enough

Birds need to stock up on food in the early evening so they can maintain their body temperature overnight.

during the day to get through the night, so there is a feeding frenzy in the afternoon. Likewise, at dawn, they have used up these energy levels so need to replenish them quickly.

The amount of food you supply is ultimately up to you, and it also depends on how many birds visit your garden. You will soon see how long certain foods last, and which are taken first, so you can develop your own feeding routine. Try not to let your feeders become empty, as birds may waste valuable energy in coming to visit empty feeders.

Remember to feed in moderation as excess food may attract unwanted visitors, such as mice and rats. You can always put more out when supplies run low, which is better than letting it pile up and spoil.

The menu

Garden bird feeding is currently going through a boom. Many wild bird mixes and high-energy foods, specifically formulated for wild birds, are available from pet shops or specialist bird food manufacturers (see Useful Contacts, page 80), and the choice can be overwhelming.

However, old, simple favourites go down very well with birds, and you do not have to go to great expense to make your garden a sanctuary for them. You can also experiment to see what works best in your garden and among the birds in your area.

For the dietary specifics of individual species, see Chapter 6, but here is a rundown of some of the best 'supplementary' foods to provide for wild birds to complement their natural diet.

The more of the following foods you provide, the greater variety of birds you will attract – and the better chance you have of providing a balanced diet for your garden birds.

There is a wide variety of bird feeders available.

FEEDING BIRDS

Scraps and leftovers

What better use for your mealtime leftovers than giving them to garden birds? Wild birds will eat many scraps from our plates and are certainly not too proud to do so!

Meat scraps, bacon rinds (preferably unsalted and chopped), potatoes and cheese (hard and grated) are all cheap and nutritious foods for wild birds.

You can hang up the remains of a joint of meat, which provides a lasting supply of food as the more agile species cling on and peck away. Just remember to avoid anything that is mouldy, too stale, over salty or spicy.

Scraps are a very undervalued and underprovided source of nutrition for wild birds – so think before you empty your plates into the dustbin after meals.

Peanuts

Peanuts are an excellent food to provide for wild birds because they are high in protein and oil, and they are attractive to many species.

The peanuts must be unsalted and served in plastic or wire-mesh feeders if whole. This will ensure that the birds have to peck at the nuts rather than pulling out whole nuts, which they could choke on. This is particularly important in summer when the adult birds may feed peanuts to their young if natural food, in the form of insects, is hard to come by. The supply of nuts served in feeders will also last longer!

Ideally, the peanuts you buy should be approved by the Birdfood

TOP TIP
Buying in bulk is always a more cost-effective way to feed garden birds, so think big!

Peanuts are a great favourite with many species.

TOP TIP
You can help provide birds with a natural source of calcium for producing eggs in the breeding season by providing oystershell grit in spring and summer.

Standards Association. This will mean that the nuts will be aflatoxin-free. Aflatoxin is produced by a mould that develops on peanuts in hot and humid conditions, and can be potentially fatal to birds.

Before you buy, always make sure the peanuts are suitable – and safe – for wild birds.

Fat balls and bird cakes

You can make you own fat balls and bird cakes by melting lard or suet in a saucepan, stirring in tasty morsels such as meat scraps, seeds and fruit, and allowing it to cool and harden. This combination of ingredients makes a very high-energy food source, perfect for winter feeding.

You can make your mix into any shape you wish (and be as ingenious as you like with your selection of mould), but the birds won't mind how it looks. If possible, try to provide different sizes. Bigger birds prefer a larger surface area to grip on to.

You can hang fat balls and birds cakes with a hook, or in mesh bags, and watch birds such as House Sparrows, tits – and, if you are lucky, Great Spotted Woodpeckers – clinging on.

This type of food does last quite a while because the birds can only extract a little at a time. Ground feeders such as Dunnocks, Robins, Wrens and thrushes, benefit too, as there are inevitable spillages.

Ready-made fat balls and a variety of bird bars are commonly available now, if you don't want to go to the trouble of making your own.

Bread

A few do's and don'ts with bread. Although it may be stale bread that is usually put out for the birds, try to make sure it isn't too far past its best – and certainly not mouldy. Birds can

This coconut shell stuffed with a mixture of fat and seeds provides an excellent source of food.

get ill, too! Don't provide bread during the breeding season because it can swell up and choke nestlings. In any case, it is always best to break the bread into small pieces or to crumble it up.

Fruit

Birds love fruit of all kinds. Apples and pears from the autumn crop can be stored and put out for the birds during winter. Raisins and sultanas make a tasty treat, too.

Hanging up half a coconut, with the fruit still intact, will provide a

DID YOU KNOW?

You may think that it is the same one or two Blue Tits coming to your feeders each day, but studies have shown that multiplying the number of birds present at any one time by 10, gives you an idea of the actual number visiting.

FEEDING BIRDS

lasting and attractive food source for birds. Never feed dessicated coconut, which can swell up after it has been eaten.

Seeds and grains

These form a large part of the natural diet of many birds, so they are an excellent food to provide in the garden.

There are now many specially formulated seed mixes available for wild birds. Some provide maximum nutrition at different times of the year, so you can buy 'summer mixes' and 'winter mixes'. Ask your supplier for advice.

There is usually a variety of ingredients in these mixes, but you can also feed individual seed and grains, including:

TOP TIP

Seeds that germinate as a result of spillages from feeders and bird-tables can be an unwelcome by-product of feeding garden birds. Position your feeders over concrete to avoid this problem.

- **Nyjer seed**
The seed of the ramtil plant. It is popular with finches and is high in oil content.

- **Millet**
- **Oatmeal**
- **Maize**
- **Sunflower seeds.**
Sunflower seeds are a great favourite with wild birds. You can provide those that have had the outer shell removed, so that birds do not have to

Grain and seeds, such as this nyjer seed, make up a large part of the diet for many species.

expend energy removing the husk from the hearts. Many species will eat them, including those that normally wouldn't attempt to remove outer husks, such as thrushes.

However, some birds – especially finches – are more than capable of removing the outer shell. The black sunflower seeds, with the outer husk intact, are cheaper, more cost-effective, and may last a bit longer. Try experimenting to see which variety works best in your garden.

Live food

Mealworms and waxworms can now be purchased as 'live food' – and the birds love them! They are very rich in protein and are a good food to serve in summer when adults are giving insect food to their young. Serve them in a container with steep sides so they cannot escape. Ask at your local pet shop or bird food supplier for more information on how to obtain them.

Dishing up

Selecting the right foods is only half the battle. The next step is to serve the food in the safest way for the birds. They need to be able to reach the source of the supply, and then they must be able to extract the food easily. From your point of view, you need to be able to replenish supplies easily and conveniently – and you want to make sure the feeding birds are visible so you can admire the fruits of your labours!

Bird-tables

Bird-tables are the best-known pieces of garden bird 'furniture', and they are very effective. They should be elevated (preferably on a pole) to

TOP TIP

Store your bird food in a cool, dry place such as a garage or garden shed. Old ice-cream tubs make excellent storage containers as do glass jars, and these prevent damp from spoiling the food. Try to use any bird food within three months of purchase.

15

FEEDING BIRDS

Position feeders near a window so you
can watch all the comings and goings.

keep the feeding birds safe from cats.

A covered roof is not essential,
though it will help to keep the food
dry in wet weather. However, the
birds may feel safer with a clear, all-
round view. Alternatively, you can
hang a feeding platform from a sturdy
branch, or attach it to a wall or fence
with a bracket.

The appearance of the bird-table
does not really matter, but there are
some important considerations:
• **Make sure there are small drainage
holes in the table to allow rainwater to
escape.**
• **There should also be a raised 'lip'
around the edge to prevent food being
blown away.**
• **Birds need to have cover nearby for a
quick getaway should danger loom, and
they also need a clear view to spot
danger approaching. As a happy
medium, try to position your table no
more than two metres from cover.**

You can buy ready-made bird-

tables, but a cheaper option is to
make your own from wood. Contact
the RSPB or British Trust for
Ornithology (see Useful Contacts,
page 80) for information about
making a simple bird-table.

Bird-feeders

You can hang bird-feeders in all
kinds of places, and the more you
have and the more positions you put
them in, the better chance you have
of attracting different species. More
and more species have learned how
to extract food from feeders in recent
years, so they are a must in any bird
garden. A wide variety of feeders is
available in pet shops and from bird
food specialists. The most popular
include:

Plastic, tubular seed feeders: These
have individual feeding ports at the
bottom of the tube (those at the
larger end of the scale have them all
the way up the sides), which fill up
with seed.

TOP TIP

Crumbs that build up in the bottom of the toaster make an excellent addition to your bird-table – or you can simply scatter them on the ground.

Peanut feeders: These are made of wire (occasionally plastic), which is essential, as the birds need to cling on, peck at the nuts, and take away smaller morsels rather than pulling out whole peanuts. This type of feeder generally has a removable top to enable you to replenish supplies easily. Some are wooden with a wire mesh panel on the front. The flat back allow this variety to be positioned on walls or fences.

Plastic mesh bags: These come ready supplied with peanuts, and they are popular with finches.

Other variations of bird-feeders include hanging logs with holes for food, bird 'houses', which are like miniature hanging bird-tables, and ceramic bells that you can hang and fill with bird cake mixes.

Bird-feeders can be hung from the bird-table, the washing line, from branches of a tree, or from brackets on the side of your house, garage or shed – but make sure they are well out of the reach of cats. The rules of positioning a bird-table also apply with feeders.

Most types of bird-feeder are available in various sizes. If you are attracting many birds, you may want to invest in larger feeders that can hold more food and need to be refilled less often.

Other feeding areas

Simply scattering food on the ground and around the bases of trees and bushes will also attract birds. It is the best way to cater for ground feeders, such as Dunnocks and Wrens, that are infrequent or reluctant visitors to feeders and to the bird-table.

Be a little creative in your scattering, too. Put grated cheese and fat into cracks in branches and trunks – the birds will find it.

Hygiene hint

Hygiene is very important. You will need to clean bird-feeders, bird-tables, and the areas underneath them regularly to remove old and mouldy food. Do not use chemicals – hot, soapy water will suffice. Moving your feeders and table to a new spot from time to time helps to prevent disease through the accumulation of food and droppings.

The Nuthatch may be a regular visitor if peanuts are provided.

WATER WAYS

It is easy to get carried away with providing food for birds and to forget that water is just as important. As well as the obvious need for drinking, birds also need water for bathing – a crucial part of their daily routine.

Keeping their feathers in tip-top condition and free from dirt and dust is a priority for birds at all times. Feathers are not just for flying; the downy body feathers provide insulation and they need to be well maintained in order to trap and keep warmth in.

Bathing birds aim to wet their feathers rather than soak them. If they get too wet, their flying ability is hampered momentarily, and they may become vulnerable to predators. Therefore, birds do not need a large surface area of water, nor any depth of water. They squat in the water and take a shower by flicking water over themselves, rather than submerging. The greasy skin surface and feather coatings help to protect them from saturation.

Seed-eating birds get thirsty easily and so they need to drink regularly.

A garden pond will be appreciated by many different types of wildlife.

Some birds also bathe in ants! Blackbirds and Jays can be seen doing this on lawns. They crouch down and open their wings and tail and let the ants crawl over their feathers. Sometimes they even pick ants up and place them on their feathers. The formic acid that the ants squirt as a defence helps remove parasites such as ticks from the birds' plumage.

In fact, providing water is just as important as providing the seeds for the birds to eat.

Bird-baths and ponds

There are numerous bird-baths available from garden centres. These are often ornamental in design, and they are an attractive addition to any garden.

Ponds are great for other wetland wildlife and the less vegetated, shallow edges can be utilised by drinking and bathing birds. You can create your own pond with a rubber liner, available from garden centres, and there are also plastic moulds that work well once they have been sunk into the ground (I have one of these in my garden).

You don't have to have a bird-bath or a pond to meet birds' need for water, though. You can easily make provision for the drinking and bathing requirements of birds yourself, if you don't want to splash out.

Plant pot saucers

For stabilising this lightweight option, place a stone in the middle of the water-filled saucer. This can also act as a perching place for the birds. You can put several all around the garden.

Birds need to keep their feathers in pristine condition.

WATER WAYS

SUMMER TIP

During droughts in summer, birds may try to bathe in water troughs and butts where they are very susceptible to drowning. If you can't cover these effectively, float a log or plank of wood in the water so birds can get to safety.

Birds, such as this Greenfinch, need access to shallow water for drinking and for bathing.

Dustbin lid

An old, shallow dustbin lid makes a very effective drinking and bathing spot for birds, and its portability is an added bonus.

You can experiment and move it easily if it doesn't seem to be attracting birds in one spot. You can sink it into the ground, or even perch it on posts, stones or bricks.

Safety first

The birds' safety is a key point when it comes to providing bathing and drinking areas. They may be at risk of drowning if the water is too deep, or, in particular, if the sides are too steep and slippery for them to get out. Birds are much less mobile when their plumage is wet.

To overcome this potential hazard,

Make sure the birds have access to water during freeze-ups. This means breaking the ice on bird-baths, ponds or any other 'watering devices' in the morning, or pouring hot water on the ice to melt it. Floating a tennis ball in ponds can also help to prevent ice-ups.

ensure there are shallow sides to your water feature and a grippy, non-slip surface to enable the birds to hold on with their claws. A layer of stones or gravel in the bottom, and a large stone in the middle, can help.

The positioning of your bird-bath is very important, too. Place it near to cover to encourage shyer species and to give the birds an easy getaway. Do not position it in spots where cats can lurk and pounce easily.

The water must be clean and fresh, so you will need to replace it regularly. Check that the water is between 2-10 cm in depth to allow a variety of species to bathe.

In icy periods, you may need to pour hot water into your bird bath.

DID YOU KNOW?

Birds don't just bathe in water. Small birds take regular dust baths in flowerbeds and other dry areas. House Sparrows love to dust bathe and several may join together for a communal bath.

RAISING YOUNG

Erecting a nest-box – or several if you have room – is a great way to make your garden attractive to nesting birds. Nest-boxes can be particularly important if natural nesting sites, in the form of trees and bushes, are scarce.

Nest-boxes are sold in many retail outlets, such as garden centres and pet shops, and by the garden bird equipment specialists (see Useful Contacts, page 80). Different types cater for different species, so it may be worth seeing what species are already present in your garden, and then selecting and putting up boxes that are suitable for them.

Broadly speaking, there are two types of box and these differ mainly in the entrance:

The open-fronted box

This has the top half of the rectangular panel at the front cut away.

The hole-entrance box

This has a round entrance hole cut into the front panel.

All nest-boxes should be well constructed and made from wood that has not been painted or treated with harmful preservatives. A perch at the entrance is not necessary, and may even encourage mammal predators such as grey squirrels and weasels.

There are also Swift, Swallow and House Martin nest-boxes that can be

Nest-box users

Open-fronted
Robin
Wren
Spotted Flycatcher
Pied Wagtail

Hole-entrance
Great Tit
Blue Tit
Coal Tit
Starling
House Sparrow
Nuthatch
Tree Sparrow

Open-fronted nest-box.

Hole-entrance nest-box.

Birds, such as this Robin, are adaptable creatures, and many species will be happy to make their home in a nest-box. This is an open-fronted box

23

RAISING YOUNG

The front of the nest box must not face south, or it will be too hot for chicks such as this Nuthatch.

placed under the eaves of your house.

The other really important factor when choosing a nest-box is the size of the entrance hole for hole-fronted nest-boxes. The basic shape and size of both main types of box is generally the same.

The entrance hole must be:

- **25 mm in diameter for Blue and Coal Tits**
- **28 mm for Great Tits and Tree Sparrows**
- **32 mm for House Sparrows and Nuthatches**
- **45 mm (in a larger box) for Starlings.**

Siting a nest-box

The positioning of a nest-box is very important, and requires a lot of thought. There are several points to consider when it comes to the well-being of the eggs and nestlings once they are in the box:
- Make sure the front does not face

south. The sun can make it very hot inside the box, and this can be fatal to nestlings.
• If possible, select a shaded position.
• Westerly winds can be cold and wet, so avoid an exposed westerly site. Ideally, position the nest-box with the front facing between north and east.
• Minimise exposure to the wind by placing the nest-box on the leeward side of a tree.
• Consider where water will flow down the trunk, and then tilt the box

slightly forward to discourage rainwater from building up.
• Place the nest-box out of reach of cats, and try not to make it too obvious to other predators, such as Magpies and grey squirrels.
• Make sure the nest-box is a sufficient height from the ground – between 2 and 5 metres is a reasonable guideline.
• Ensure the nest-box is securely fastened to avoid any disasters once the birds take up residence.
• Open-fronted nest-boxes are best placed in cover – partially hidden among plants and foliage. This gives them protection from predators, and will also offer young birds greater safety as they make their first uncertain flight from the nest. They may well need something close by to fall back on – literally!

Do it yourself
Nest-boxes are readily available, but you may prefer to make your own. Contact the RSPB or BTO (see Useful Contacts) for a basic nest-box plan.
You can make a box that has a removable upper panel (with an entrance hole) that can easily transform into an open-fronted nest-box, if you find that one style is not being used by the birds in your garden.

Birds, such as this Blue Tit, will make use of all sorts of different material when building a nest

RAISING YOUNG

Nesting material

You can give nesting birds a helping hand by putting out nesting material for them. Human hair, wool and scraps of fabric all make perfect materials for nest-building. You can even offer the material in a hanging feeder so that the birds can extract it. Alternatively, scatter it over branches or on the ground.

Once the box is up, your work is done and you can watch as birds come to investigate it. Remember to put the box up well in advance of the breeding season – the winter is the perfect time. If you wait for a warm spring day, the birds will already have settled elsewhere!

Clean up

Once you are sure that your garden birds have finished nesting and are not planning another brood (see Chapter 6 for information on the number of broods produced by each species), it is a good idea to give the box a clean, and to make any repairs that may be necessary. Do this in late autumn or early winter.

Remove any nesting material, as it may contain parasites, and then clean the inside with hot, soapy water and allow it to dry. There is no need to take the box down for winter, but

TOP TIP

A nest-box attached to a wall is perfectly acceptable, and you know the box will be safe from cats.

If you do not have trees in your garden, you can fix the nest-box to a wall.

make sure it remains in good condition. By leaving it in place, the birds will come to accept it as a natural part of the garden. In winter, nest-boxes are also used as roosting sites by some birds.

DID YOU KNOW?

The number of eggs per clutch tends to be smaller in second and third broods for most species of birds.

TOP TIP

If you have large trees in your garden, and you know that Tawny Owls are present in your area, you may consider putting up a Tawny Owl box. Old tea chests with one end open, securely fastened in a tree, are perfect.

GARDENING FOR BIRDS

Birds, such as this Chaffinch, will make use of trees and shrubs as natural cover.

By providing supplementary food, water and nest-boxes, you are well on the way to having a really good bird garden. However, there is still plenty more you can do.

Implementing a few, simple measures with birds in mind, as you plan, plant, and manage your garden, can make a huge contribution to the well-being of your garden birds, and may help to attract even more.

You can create natural nesting and roosting sites for birds by providing cover. By planting trees and shrubs that have berries and attract insects, you are enhancing the food supply for birds, as well as attracting a range of other wildlife. You will be surprised to find how easy it is – and how just a few provisions can make a world of difference.

A wildflower garden

Plants that are frequently discarded as 'weeds' by gardeners are very valuable for birds, so try to think of them in their real guise of wildflowers instead. Many are beautiful to look at, in addition to their numerous benefits to wildlife. They provide natural food for birds in the form of their seeds and the insects they attract.

Why not set aside part of your garden as a wildflower patch? You can buy wildflower mixes from your local garden centre, and, as well as providing a bit of diversity to your garden flora, birds will really welcome it.

A garden doesn't have to be overrun with wildflowers (you can control their spread), and you certainly don't have to have a 'messy' garden to make it attractive to birds. Just remember not to be too tidy. Leave a patch of wildflowers here and there, and leave the seed heads on flowers throughout the autumn and winter. If you are concerned about the plants setting seed, collect the seeds and put them out on the bird-table.

Here is a selection of native wildflowers that are great for insects, provide seeds for birds, and will also make an attractive addition to any garden.

Red campion
White campion
Primrose
Bramble
Teasel
Spear thistle
Foxglove
Stinging nettle
White dead nettle
Herb Robert
Native grasses
Docks
Chickweed.

Trees and shrubs

Not all gardens have the space for trees and shrubs, but if you do, then go for it! Looking after your birds during the day with food and water is crucial, but it is important to remember what happens to them at night.

Wildflowers attract insects as well as providing seed – two important types of food for birds.

GARDENING FOR BIRDS

A good night's sleep is as vital to birds as it is to us! They need to conserve energy and need somewhere safe to roost where they will not be disturbed.

Thick cover keeps them hidden from predators and helps to retain warmth. If they can find it in the garden, they do not need to expend energy seeking it elsewhere.

Many birds build their nests within trees and bushes, so you can also help to provide 'natural' nest sites by planting a few. As well as the obvious perching posts, nest sites and roosting places for garden birds, trees and shrubs provide food in the form of fruits, berries and seeds and, like wildflowers, attract many insects for birds to feed on.

Here are some of the best trees and shrubs – mainly native species – that are suitable for gardens and that are very attractive to garden birds.

Teasel is an attractive choice for a wildflower garden, and will be appreciated by birds such as this Goldfinch.

Blackbirds, and many other birds, will feast on berries.

Ivy

Some gardeners worry that ivy can take over, but you can keep it under control with regular pruning. Ivy produces berries, which often last well into the winter, and these are a welcome source of food for birds.

The flowers that are produced attract many flying insects in the autumn, including bees, wasps, flies, moths, butterflies, hoverflies and many more.

Ivy is an evergreen, so it can provide much welcome cover for birds in winter. Many birds also build their nests within it.

Honeysuckle

An attractive climber, with a sweet scent, which attracts insects. It can provide thick cover when mature.

Silver birch

An elegant tree, which is excellent for attracting insects, and the silver bark is a pleasing addition to any garden. The catkins it produces may attract Siskins and Lesser Redpolls.

TOP TIP

Plant sunflowers and let them go to seed naturally. You can collect the seed and then put it out through the winter for the birds, or leave them alone and let birds visit the flowerheads and extract the seed themselves.

GARDENING FOR BIRDS

Red berry bearers

Rowan, dog rose and guelder rose produce excellent crops in autumn and winter, and, unlike many berry-bearing shrubs, they are true natives. Dog rose produces rose hips rather than berries.

Elder

Not to be confused with the alder (a waterside tree), the purple-black berries are an excellent food source for birds in the autumn.

Holly

A great shrub for nesting birds – many garden species make their nests within the spiny foliage of mature bushes. Berries provide colour in the

A pile of dead and rotting logs makes a great home for insects.

> Try to have at least one evergreen shrub in the garden, as they provide roosting cover throughout the year. Conifers are often frowned upon because of their extensive underground root systems and the great height to which they can grow. But if you have the space, they are welcomed by birds as nesting and roosting sites.

winter, and food for birds. It is an evergreen, and so it also has roosting attractions for birds in winter.

Hawthorn & blackthorn

These are the classic hedgerow shrubs of the British countryside. Their thorns and thick cover in spring and summer make them good nesting bushes for birds, and the berries will be welcomed by garden birds in autumn and winter.

Bird cherry & crab apple

The fruits of these trees are not the most appetizing to humans, but birds love them. They are also good insect trees.

Buddleia

The 'butterfly bush' is not strictly native, although it is naturalised in many parts of Britain. In both white and lilac forms, it is extremely attractive to butterflies and other insects. I once counted 120 butterflies (of half a dozen species) on the four bushes in my garden.

Windfall fruit provides a tasty treat for this Starling.

Cotoneaster
This non-native evergreen is another excellent shrub that produces a large crop of berries.

Box
This evergreen is a scarce native, but is widely planted. It provides good, thick cover and is often infested with aphids.

Fruit trees
Most fruit-producing trees will provide food for birds (especially when the fruit is ripe and fallen).

The ripe fruit is also irresistible to insects.

GO PESTICIDE-FREE
Avoid using pesticides in the garden. By killing off insects, you are killing off bird food. Slugs can be controlled by putting out a saucer of beer. You can then remove the 'drunk' slugs to a more welcome location. Remember that hedgehogs love slugs and that many birds also eat them. Natural predators such as ladybirds will help control unwanted pests such as greenfly and blackfly. The best pest controllers in the garden are often birds, so by attracting them, you can also keep down the numbers of pests.

CHAPTER 6

ALL ABOUT YOUR BIRDS

O nce you see birds in your garden on a regular basis, you will want to be able to identify the different species, pick out the males from the females, and spot the young birds. The ID challenge that birds present is one of the most enjoyable aspects of garden bird watching.

Here is a guide to the most regular garden visitors – all of which you can attract by following the advice in this book. I have included some useful tips so you can recognise the birds by sight and by sound, as well as by the way they behave.

There are also notes on each species' nesting habits and feeding preferences, so you can cater for individual needs.

The distinctive-looking Bullfinch is one of the easier birds to recognise.

Identification

A very colourful bird, with a striking face pattern of red, white and black bands. The name comes from the golden yellow panel in the black and white wings. The Goldfinch has a long, pale, pointy beak and a brown back. Young birds can be confusing, as they have a plain face. As the autumn advances, they gain the distinctive face pattern. Males and females are alike.

Voice

Goldfinches twitter constantly to one another in a series of cheerful, buzzing, twittering notes, which also forms most of their song.

Feeding preferences

Small seeds. Teasels and thistles are favourites, and insects are consumed in summer. Sunflower and nyjer seeds, and peanuts, are good supplementary foods to provide in the garden.

Nesting habits

Builds a compact, well-hidden cup nest of moss, roots and grass, lined with wool, hair, and, occasionally, feathers. Lays 4-6 glossy, pale blue eggs with reddish marks in each clutch – 2, rarely 3, broods.

Look out for...

Goldfinches balancing expertly on the heads of flowers, using their fine beaks like tweezers to extract seeds.

Did you know?

Flocks of Goldfinches are known as 'charms' – a great name, as there is no more charming sight than a flock of these multi-coloured gems in the garden.

CHAFFINCH

Identification
The male Chaffinch (pictured) is extremely colourful, with pink underparts and face, a blue cap, brown back, and black and white wings. The female is trickier to identify, and her brown appearance may invite confusion with the female House Sparrow. The key is to look at the black and white wing. Both sexes have a 'peaked' head. The Chaffinch often shuffles along on the ground like a clockwork toy.

Voice
A cheerful 'pink' and low-pitched 'chup'. The song is a loud, rattling verse, which ends with a flourish.

Feeding preferences
Mostly vegetable matter, with seeds predominant. Also eats insects, spiders and earthworms.

Seed mixes, sunflower hearts, bread and cheese are favourite garden foods.

Nesting habits
The nest is a neat cup incorporating moss, hair, feathers, grass and lichens, usually positioned in the fork of a tree or bush.

Lays 3-5 eggs, ranging from blue-green to reddish grey with 'scribbled' markings, in a single brood.

Look out for...
Chaffinches performing flycatching sorties from trees in summer, flashing their black and white wings.

Did you know?
The perky Chaffinch is one of the commonest birds in Britain and actually outnumbers the House Sparrow.

GREENFINCH

Identification

It is only the male Greenfinch that is truly green, and he has just as much yellow in his plumage – with prominent flashes in the wing and on the tail. Females (pictured) and young birds are browner and greyer, but the yellow flashes are a giveaway.

Voice

Song is a varied, almost canary-like twitter with frequent wheezy interjections. Call is a short 'juit'.

Feeding preferences

Seeds, berries and fruit tree buds with some insects and beetles in summer. The Greenfinch is a true acrobat that is at home on hanging tubes and mesh-feeders offering seeds and peanuts, as well as on bird-tables.

Nesting habits

The nest has a base of twigs, grass, moss and lichen, and is lined with grass, roots, hair and feathers. It is built against a tree trunk or in a sturdy fork of a dense bush; often in conifers. Generally, 4-6 eggs per clutch, and 2-3 broods.

Look out for...

The Greenfinch's amazing display flight in spring. Males patrol above their territory with a peculiar bat-like display flight, featuring slow-motion wingbeats, and erratic twists and turns.

The males sing and call at the same time to make absolutely sure any females in the vicinity take notice!

BULLFINCH

Identification
The male (pictured) of this stout, chunky finch is bright red below, with a black cap and silver wings and back. The female is a rather washed-out version of the male. Young birds lack the black cap of the adults. In flight, a square white rump patch may catch your eye. Remember that the stocky Bullfinch is 'bull-necked'.

Voice
Calls with a soft, ringing 'piuh'. The song contains this note, and a variety of hesitant, squeaky notes. It is rarely heard, as it is so indistinct and quiet.

Feeding preferences
Seeds and berries. Feeds caterpillars to its young. In spring, nibbles on tender buds and shoots of shrubs and fruit trees.

The Bullfinch is less likely to come to supplementary offerings than other finches, but you may tempt it with seed, sunflower hearts and black sunflower seeds.

Nesting habits
Builds its nest of thin twigs, moss and lichens, lined with fine roots, in thick hedges. Lays 4-5 eggs in each clutch – usually 2 broods.

Look out for...
Roaming family parties coming into the garden in the summer.

Identification

An attractive small, green, yellow, black and white finch with a small, spiky beak and short, forked tail. Males (pictured) have a black cap and chin; females and young birds are plainer faced and more streaky below.

Voice

The main call is a ringing 'tsu' interspersed with harder twittering notes. The song is a pleasant twitter, ending with a 'creaky door' note.

Feeding preferences

Mainly seeds of trees. In the garden, the Siskin shows a liking for peanuts in plastic, red mesh-feeders. It may be that the red bags remind them of their natural pinecone food. Sunflower and nyjer seed may also entice them.

Nesting habits

Usually builds its nest of twigs, lichens and moss, lined with down and hair, in a large conifer. 3-5 eggs per clutch, 2 broods.

Look out for...

Flocks of Siskins dangling upside down from the catkins and cones produced by pine, alder and birch trees.

Did you know?

Siskins often come into gardens during wet weather when pinecones in coniferous forests close up and they cannot reach the seeds inside.

BRAMBLING

Identification

Males have a jet-black head in spring and summer, but in winter this remains as a 'scaly' black. Breast and shoulders are orange, the wings are black and white, and the belly is white, spotted with a little black. The female (pictured) is very like a female Chaffinch, but look out for the telltale orange on the breast and shoulders. The Brambling has a narrow white rump, which helps to identify it in flight.

Voice

Unlikely to be heard singing in Britain. Calls include a hard 'tek' note (shorter and sharper than the Chaffinch's 'chup'), and a wheezy 'dweee'.

Feeding preferences

Seed and sunflower mix may attract Bramblings to bird-tables, and on the ground, where they often join Chaffinches.

Look out for...

Sightings of this attractive finch between late September and April. Very occasionally pairs nest in Scotland, but it is strictly a winter visitor elsewhere.

Did you know?

If the beechmast crop fails in northern Europe, Bramblings may come here in their millions in search of food. After they have eaten the beechmast, many come into gardens.

WREN

Identification
The brown Wren's tiny size, 'ball-shaped body' and stumpy, often-cocked tail is distinctive. It is barred below, has a white stripe over each eye, and has quite a long beak in proportion to the rest of its body. Sexes are alike.

Voice
Calls are a hard, piercing 'zek' and a rattling trill when excited. The song is incredibly loud for such a small bird and is a rapid burst of varied, musical warbling, starting suddenly and finishing abruptly.

Nesting habits
The nest is a dome of moss, leaves and grass. Lays 5-8 red-spotted white eggs per clutch – 2 broods. The Wren will use open-fronted nest boxes. Male Wrens may build as many as 8 nests for their mate to choose from.

Feeding preferences
Mainly insects, spiders and seeds. Grated cheese, mealworms and oats are garden favourites.

Look out for...
Watch a singing Wren closely. Because of the effort it puts in, you will really see its tiny body vibrate!

Did you know?
During cold winter weather, Wrens will roost together and huddle up to help conserve their body heat. Nest-boxes are often selected as roost sites – 49 Wrens were once counted entering a single box!

ROBIN

Identification

The Robin's red breast ensures it is one of the best known and easiest of garden birds to recognise. Male and female are virtually identical. Young birds are harder to identify as they lack the red breast.

Voice

The song is rather mournful – a soft but varied warbling. The call is a single, quiet, ticking note.

Feeding preferences

Mainly insects, plus seeds, fruit and berries. Mealworms, oats, bread and grated cheese are garden favourites.

Nesting habits

The nest is a cup of leaves, moss and grass, often built near to the ground.

Lays 5-6 whitish eggs with red spots per clutch – 2 (rarely 3) broods. A frequent user of open-fronted nest-boxes.

Look out for...

Rival Robins from neighbouring territories squaring up to one another. The red breast acts as a warning to stay away, and the birds proudly puff out their chests to show off to maximum effect. If the intruder still does not back down, the birds will often fight.

Did you know?

Robins are eccentric nesters and some pairs build their nest in bizarre places, ranging from inside pockets of old coats hanging up in sheds to abandoned kettles!

DUNNOCK

Identification

An easy bird to overlook, as it shuffles quietly along on the ground near to cover. The Dunnock is soberly coloured and featureless at first glance, but take a closer look and you will see an attractive blue-grey head and underparts, set against a black-striped brown back and wings. Males, females, and juveniles are similar.

Voice

The Dunnock's song is a pleasant but slightly scratchy warble. The call is a ringing 'chay' note, often uttered several times in succession when alarmed.

Feeding preferences

Insects form the bulk of its natural diet. Small fragments of food, such as bread, oats, cheese, and 'fall out' from bird cake mix, are preferred by garden visitors.

Nesting habits

A cup nest of leaves, grass and roots hidden in a bush. Lays 4-6 blue eggs per clutch – 2-3 broods per year.

Look out for...

Fascinating mating behaviour in spring. Female Dunnocks often mate with multiple males (and vice versa), and she may sneak off from her regular partner if another male enters her territory – so the male has to be on his guard!

Did you know?

The Dunnock used to be known as the 'Hedge Sparrow' and, indeed, it is still called this by many people. However, it is not a real sparrow – it is a member of a family of birds known as the accentors.

NUTHATCH

Identification

Orange below and blue-grey above, with a big black stripe through each eye and down behind each cheek. The Nuthatch has a chisel-like bill and a short tail making it look rather 'front heavy'. Sexes are alike. It is rarely found far from mature trees.

Voice

Chief calls are a loud, metallic 'chwit-chwit', a shrill 'twee, twee', and a rapid, piping trill.

Feeding preferences

Acorns, nuts, seeds and insects. The Nuthatch can be attracted into gardens with peanuts, seed mixes and fat balls and cakes.

Nesting habits

The nest is built in a bark-and-leaf-lined hole in a large branch or tree trunk. However, the Nuthatch will use hole-fronted nest-boxes sited in larger gardens with mature trees. Lays 6-11 eggs in a single clutch.

Look out for...

Nuthatches taking items of food and then wedging them into cracks in bark, to hammer them open with their bills.

Did you know?

The Nuthatch can walk head-first down tree trunks as well as climbing upwards – a unique feat!

Identification

Despite its name, only the adult male Blackbird is black. Females are brown, as are the young birds (pictured), which can be recognised by their short-tailed and scaly appearance. The male also has a bright orange beak and eye ring.

Blackbirds are often found hopping around on lawns, looking inquisitive and confident.

Voice

A lovely, melodic song. The alarm call is a chinking single note, uttered repeatedly, and the flight call is a chuckling rattle.

Feeding preferences

Worms, fruit, berries, seeds, insects and spiders. The Blackbird take a variety of garden bird food from the ground or bird-table.

Nesting habits

Cup nest containing twigs, moss, grass and roots, built in a bush or tree and lined with grass. Lays 3-5 greenish-blue eggs per clutch – 2-3 broods (rarely 4).

Did you know?

Blackbirds are faithful mates and pairs often re-form in successive breeding seasons.

SONG THRUSH

Identification

The heavily black-spotted white underparts and brown upperparts should enable you to recognise this much-declined garden bird. It is smaller, browner and shyer than the Mistle Thrush. Sexes are alike; young are very spotty above.

Voice

A beautiful song, with a variety of phrases, that is delivered from a high perch. The call is a clipped 'tsip'.

Feeding preferences

Slugs, snails, berries and fruit, but will take a variety of garden bird food from the ground or bird-table.

Nesting habits

Song Thrushes build a cup nest of twigs, grass and moss, in a tree or bush. The nest is lined with mud.

Generally lays 3-5 blue, lightly speckled eggs per clutch – 2-3 broods per year (rarely 4).

Look out for...

Song Thrushes using 'anvils' to break open the shells of snails. The bird holds the snail in its beak and smashes it against a large stone.

Many individual birds may have a regular stone and the ground around it can become littered with snail shells.

MISTLE THRUSH

Identification

A bigger, bolder, greyer and more heavily-spotted version of the Song Thrush. It has white outer tail feathers, unlike the Song Thrush, and the underwing is brilliant white – both useful in-flight pointers. Sexes are alike and the young are very scaly.

Voice

A pleasant and wild, far-carrying song, lacking the variety and pace of the Song Thrush. The flight and alarm call is like a football rattle.

Feeding preferences

Fruits and berries, worms, insects and spiders. Plant a berry bush in the garden to attract feeding birds, or provide fallen fruit on the ground

Nesting habits

A root-and-moss-based nest is lined with grass and decorated with lichens, feathers and bits of wool.It is built in a fork of a tree – sometimes on a branch – at great height. Lays 2-6 cream or greenish-blue eggs per clutch. 2 broods.

Look out for...

Bullying behaviour. The Mistle Thrush is our largest thrush and is very protective of its nesting territory and berry-bearing bushes. It can be seen in high speed chases, 'escorting' intruders away.

Did you know?

The Mistle Thrush is also called the 'stormcock' because of its habit of singing before, after, and even during rainstorms!

REDWING

Identification
Don't be confused by the name. The red is actually under the wing and on the flanks. Song Thrush-sized, speckled below, with a prominent stripe over each eye and under each cheek, and a yellow-based beak. Sexes are alike.

Voice
Unlikely to be heard singing in British gardens. The call is a high pitched 'seeh'.

Feeding preferences
Attracted into gardens with berry-bearing trees and shrubs. Putting out fruit such as apples and pears will also work, especially during hard weather.

Look out for...
Sightings of this small thrush between mid-September and April. A few pairs may nest in Scotland, but generally it is a winter visitor.

Did you know?
The Redwings that spend winter here come from two areas: Scandinavia and Iceland.

Identification

A big, bold thrush, similar in size and shape to the Mistle Thrush. It has the typical spotted thrush breast, but the back and wings are a chocolate brown, and the head and rump are grey-blue. The tail is black. Sexes alike. The Fieldfare may appear wary.

Voice

Contact call is a series of 'chack, chack, chack' notes, with a few wheezy notes in-between. Unlikely to be heard singing in British gardens.

Feeding preferences

During its winter residence in Britain, the Fieldfare feeds on a variety of berries (native and ornamental), plus fruit.

It also feeds on worms that it pulls from the ground in pastureland and fields.

Look out for...

Sightings of this striking thrush between October and early April.

Did you know?

A few pairs of Fieldfare attempt to nest in Scotland each year, but it is strictly a winter visitor from Scandinavia in the rest of the country.

COAL TIT

Identification

The Coat Tit has a black head with white cheeks, like the Great Tit, but the white patch on the back of the head instantly identifies this, our smallest, tit. It lacks the yellow in its plumage that is typical of the Blue and Great Tit, and is buff below and darker brown above. Sexes alike.

Voice

Call is a piping 'tsuee'. The song is a repetitive rendition of a ringing double note.

Feeding preferences

Food is mainly insects, but it will take many supplementary garden foods, such as peanuts, seeds, bird cakes and fat balls.

Nesting habits

A moss-and-feather-based nest is built in a hole in an old tree stump or tree. Lays 7-11 white eggs in a single brood. Occasionally uses hole-fronted nest-boxes.

Look out for...

Hoarding behaviour. Coal Tits often grab an item of food and then vanish with it. They hoard the food nearby, and will consume it in peace later on.

Did you know?

There is a 'pecking order' among the tits, and the Coal Tit, being the smallest species, comes at the bottom and is frequently ousted out by Great and Blue Tits.

LONG-TAILED TIT

Identification
Like a spoon or a lollipop in shape, due to its tiny, round head and body, and very long tail. The Long-tailed Tit is black and white, with a rosy tint to parts of the plumage. Sexes are alike; the young have dark sides to their heads.

Voice
A spluttering, single note contact call, and a high-pitched 'si, si, si'.

Feeding preferences
Mainly insects with occasional seeds and spiders. The Long-tailed Tit will visit fat balls, bird cakes, and peanut feeders.

Nesting habits
Builds an amazing domed nest, like a fluffy ball, in a bush. It is made from moss, feathers and spider webs. The outside is coated with grey lichens for camouflage. Lays 8-12 white (some speckled with red) eggs in a single brood.

Look out for...
The male's brothers helping to feed his brood if their own breeding attempts have failed.

Did you know?
A single Long-tailed Tit nest can contain up to 2,000 feathers!

BLUE TIT

Identification

This tiny bird is a colourful mix of blue on the head and wings, green on the back, yellow below, with a black-striped white face. This is the only tit with a blue cap. Agile and acrobatic in its movements, it is rarely still for long. Males and females are very similar, although the male has more white on its forehead. The young are rather washed out and yellow-cheeked.

Voice

A variety of high-pitched calls. The song is a rapid, liquid trill.

Feeding preferences

Mainly insects and spiders, plus fruit, grain, seed and buds. The Blue Tit has a fondness for caterpillars in spring, and it raises its young on these. Peanuts and sunflower seeds are a real attraction in the garden, as are fat balls and bird cakes.

Nesting habits

A hole-fronted nestbox regular. Natural nest sites are holes in trees. The cavity is padded with moss and grass and is lined with hair and feathers by the female. Lays 7-12 white, red-brown spotted eggs per clutch. Single brooded.

Look out for...

Overworked parents. A pair of Blue Tits may visit the nest up to 1,000 times a day, with single items of food for their young.

Did you know?

During winter, a Blue Tit spends up to 85 per cent of its time feeding.

Identification
As its name suggests, the Great Tit is the largest of the tit family in Britain. It has a black head with white cheeks; yellow below, with a striking, black line extending from the throat down the belly. The sexes are similar, but the male has a more solid black line down the breast. The young are washed out versions of the adults, with yellow cheeks.

Voice
Has an incredibly wide vocabulary – More than 300 different calls have been described! The commonest notes are 'tee-cha, tee-cha'.

Feeding preferences
Exactly the same as the Blue Tit.

Nesting habits
A hole-fronted nest-box regular that uses moss, grass, hair and feather-lined holes in trees as natural sites. The Great Tit lays 3-18 white, red-spotted eggs in a single clutch (rarely two).

Look out for...
Great Tits 'song-duelling' in late winter and spring. Rival males try to outdo each other in an attempt to attract a female.

GOLDCREST

Identification

Europe's smallest bird is a true midget. Weighing just a few grams and measuring only 8.5 cm from bill to tail tip, the Goldcrest can be identified on size alone. You need to look carefully to see the black-bordered, golden yellow crest. This is more orange in the male.

Voice

A very high-pitched, quiet 'see, see, see', which is inaudible to some. The song is a shrill warble, ending with a little trill.

Feeding preferences

Insects in the main, which it finds on the undersides of leaves and especially pine needles. The Goldcrest may be tempted into quieter areas of the garden if you scatter small food fragments in trees and bushes.

Nesting habits

The moss nest, woven together with spider webs and lined with feathers, is normally suspended under thick foliage – frequently in evergreens. Lays 7-10 white to pale brown eggs per clutch. Double-brooded.

Look out for...

When alarmed, excited in display, or during aggressive encounters with other Goldcrests, they raise up their crests.

Identification

A tiny, mainly featureless bird with spindly black legs, and a thin bill. The plumage is essentially brown with a few green and yellow tints, especially in the breeding season. Sexes and juveniles are alike.

Voice

This warbler gets its name from its song – a repetitive 'chiff-chaff, chiff-chaff'. The call is a cheerful 'hweet'.

Feeding preferences

Chiefly insects, but the Chiffchaff will take a variety of scraps and fruit from bird-tables, as well as berries in autumn and winter.

Nesting habits

Builds a spherical nest of leaves, moss, and stalks, lined with feathers, and positioned low to the ground in thick cover. Lays 4-7 eggs per clutch – 2 broods in the south.

Did you know?

Chiffchaffs were once exclusively a summer visitor from Africa, but now large numbers spend winter here. Many seek shelter and food in gardens.

BLACKCAP

Identification
Only the male has a black cap. Females (pictured) and juveniles have a red-brown cap, which stops just above the eye. The rest of the plumage is grey. They are small birds with spindly legs, and spiky bills.

Voice
A short, sharp, single 'tac'. The song is a pleasant, musical warbling.

Feeding preferences
Insects, fruit and berries. The Blackcap is fond of apples on the bird-table, but will also take a variety of food fragments from seeds to suet.

Nesting habits
Root and grass nest, often lined with horsehair, built in bushes and hedgerows. Lays 3-6 eggs – often double-brooded in the south.

Did you know?
Like the Chiffchaff, the Blackcap was once only a summer visitor to Britain from Africa. Now large numbers of birds that nested in Europe spend winter here.

GREAT SPOTTED WOODPECKER

Identification

This thrush-sized woodpecker has a big, strong chisel-like bill, and a short but strong tail for balancing on trees. Much of the plumage is black and white; males and young birds (pictured) have a red patch on their head. The Great Spotted Woodpecker has a distinctive, 'undulating' style of flying.

Voice

The call is a piercing 'kik' and also has a harsh chatter. It drums on trees with its beak to mark the boundaries of its territory, and to attract a mate in late winter and spring.

Feeding preferences

The Great Spotted Woodpecker is omnivorous in its diet. As well as eating the larvae of wood-boring insects and nuts, seeds and berries, it will take young birds and eggs during the breeding season, as well as consuming a variety of insects. This colourful woodpecker has learned how to extract peanuts from feeders, and can also cling to larger fat balls.

Nesting habits

Pairs excavate their own nest hole and chamber in trees, using their powerful beaks. The nest has just a few wood chips as a lining. Lays 4-7 white eggs in a single brood.

Look out for...

Great Spotted Woodpeckers drumming on telegraph poles – which has caused a few concerns for phone companies!

Did you know?

Great Spotted Woodpeckers have specially reinforced skulls to enable them to cope with drumming. They can make 14 strikes per second with their beaks.

GREEN WOODPECKER

Identification

The only greeny-yellow bird of this size likely to visit gardens. The Green Woodpecker has a large, sturdy beak, strong feet and a long, strong tail for balance. The back and wings are bright green, and the red crown is very striking. Males have a red 'moustache', females have a black moustache.

It shows a very striking yellow rump and back as it flies up. Juveniles (pictured) are spotted black below. Unusually for a woodpecker, it is as much at home on the ground as it is in trees, but it is a shy and wary bird.

Voice

A far-carrying 'yaffling' call, which sounds as if the bird is laughing.

Feeding preferences

The Green Woodpecker's main food is the larvae of wood-boring insects and ants.

The best ways to attract these birds is to encourage ants to live in your garden, and to keep the lawn well mown so that they can come to feed on their favourite food there.

Nesting habits

Pairs bore a nest hole into the trunk of a tree. The only lining is a few wood chips in the bottom. Lays 5-9 white eggs per clutch. Single-brooded.

Did you know?

The Green Woodpecker has a tremendously long tongue, which it probes into the ground in search of ants. The tongue is coated with a sticky saliva and has a barbed tip.

Identification

The most colourful member of the crow family, the Jay is shy by nature and prefers to keep to cover. Essentially pink, black and white, with a black-flecked white crest which can be raised. The Jay has broad wings and a rather 'floppy' flight, when it displays a white rump patch and electric blue wing panels. Sexes are alike.

Voice

A harsh, discordant screech.

Feeding preferences

Mainly vegetable matter, such as fruits and acorns, but will also eat young birds and eggs, slugs, worms and insects. The Jay may visit peanut feeders and bird-tables occasionally.

Try putting some bird cake mix in the branches of trees to tempt this shy bird into the garden.

Nesting habits

A stick and twig nest, lined with roots and earth, is built in undergrowth and trees. Jays lay 5-6 eggs per clutch. Single-brooded.

Look out for...

Jays hoarding acorns. They collect acorns in autumn and bury them for a readily-available source of food during winter. This is how many oak trees germinate.

Did you know?

Jays watch others to see where they bury their acorns so they can steal them when their backs are turned!

JACKDAW

Identification
Mostly black. The smaller size, beady eye, and especially the big grey area on its neck sides and nape, separate it from the Carrion Crow and Rook, which may occasionally visit gardens. Sexes are alike.

Voice
A loud, ringing 'chack', and a ringing 'kyow'.

Feeding preferences
A wide range of animal food, such as insects, young birds, eggs, mice, snails, slugs and worms, as well as fruit, berries and root crops.

Jackdaws will come to bird-tables and lawns to feed on a variety of scraps.

Nesting habits
Prefers to nest in wool-, hair-, fur- and grass-lined holes in a tree or building, but will build a stick nest in trees occasionally.

The Jackdaw often nests in chimney pots. Lays 4-6 eggs (often marked with black blotches) per clutch. Single-brooded.

Did you know?
Like most crows, the Jackdaw is very intelligent.

MAGPIE

Identification

The black and white plumage and very long, green-glossed tail, make the Magpie an unmistakable sight. Sexes are alike.

Voice

A harsh, rattling call and a 'babbling' song.

Feeding preferences

The Magpie is omnivorous, and will eat anything, from the eggs and chicks of other birds during the breeding season to insects such as beetles, worms, caterpillars and flies.

Nesting habits

Pairs build a prominent, dome-shaped nest of sticks in the branches of trees and shrubs. The interior is lined with mud, and there are often two entrances. Lays 3-9 pale green, spotted eggs per clutch. Single-brooded.

Did you know?

The Magpie's reputation as a jewellery thief is deserved. Crows are attracted by bright, shiny objects – and the Magpie most especially – so don't leave any valuables lying about!

STARLING

Identification

Looks all black at a distance, so it invites confusion with the male Blackbird. However, it is a smaller bird with a shaggy crest and, outside the breeding season, has white spots. Purple and green glossy tones can be seen in the plumage when the sun shines. Young birds are biscuit brown at first and gradually obtain adult-like spotty feathering. Some are a confusing mix of both for a time in late summer. Sexes are alike.

Voice

The Starling is a brilliant mimic. I have heard my local birds imitating more than 50 different species. They can also do passable imitations of man-made sounds, such as phones, road drills, and keys turning in locks!

Feeding preferences

Eats almost anything, and will accept a wide variety of supplementary food from bird-table scraps to peanuts and bread.

The Starling also clings to feeders with ease.

Nesting habits

Most nest in holes and cavities in trees and buildings. They lay 4-6 pale blue eggs per clutch – 1 brood (occasionally 2) – and will use nest-boxes.

Did you know?

The Starlings you see in your garden in winter may have come from a lot further away than you realise. Millions of immigrant Russian Starlings swell the numbers of our resident population at this time – but they are indistinguishable from 'our' birds.

HOUSE SPARROW

Identification

A cheeky, confiding bird used to living alongside man. Males have a black bib, a stripe through each eye, and a grey crown. They range from white to grey below, and the back and wings are brown, striped with black. Females and young have a faint yellowish stripe above each eye, and lack the black on the face.

Voice

A variety of chirping notes.

Feeding preferences

Grain, seed and insects. Peanuts, bird cakes and fat balls, kitchen scraps, plus any seeds will soon attract these bold birds into the garden.

Nesting habits

Nests in holes, in crevices in buildings, or in thick, creeping vegetation, such as ivy. Lays 3-5 variably coloured eggs per clutch – 3 broods.

The House Sparrow will nest in hole-fronted nest-boxes.

Look out for...

House Sparrows taking dust baths in hot weather.

SPOTTED FLYCATCHER

Identification

Plumage is essentially grey-brown with a few fine streaks on the breast. Young birds have more spots. Sexes are alike.

Voice

Calls are high-pitched, soft and indistinct; best described as a short 'zee' and a harder clicking note, sometimes combined. The song is a simple series of squeaky notes mixed with soft trills.

Feeding preferences

Solely insects.

Nesting habits

The Spotted Flycatcher will build its moss, wool and hair nest in some very strange places – from against walls to the tops of doors. It is a regular user of open-fronted nestboxes. Lays 4-5 eggs per clutch. Often 2 broods.

Look out for...

Spotted Flycatchers perching on prominent lookout posts, such as exposed branches, waiting for flies to come within striking distance, before darting out and snapping them up. The effect is very eye-catching, despite happening at rapid speed!

Did you know?

Spotted Flycatchers are one of the last migrant birds to return to Britain each spring to nest. Many do not arrive until well into May.

COLLARED DOVE

Identification
The best fieldmark of this elegant dove is the neat, white-edged black half-collar. The rest of the plumage is a pale grey-brown. The long tail has white corners, and the outer wing is black. Sexes are alike.

Voice
The call is a noisy, purring 'kreear'. The song is a series of three cooing notes ('doo-dooo-do'), repeated several times.

Feeding preferences
Spilled grain and seeds, plus some fruit and berries. Bird-table seeds are the best garden food to provide.

Nesting habits
Builds an untidy stick platform nest in trees (especially conifers), in which it lays 2 white eggs per clutch. There is a minimum of 2 broods per year.

Did you know?
The Collared Dove is a natural 'invader' from Asia. It spread across Europe to Britain and the first pair nested here in the 1950s. Now it is one of the commonest garden birds.

WOOD PIGEON

Identification

Our largest pigeon, it waddles around and often looks very well fed! Blue-grey in colour, the Wood Pigeon has a lilac breast, a green and white collar, and black-tipped grey wings with a white stripe across each one. 'Baby' pigeons are rarely seen because they are virtually fully grown before they leave the nest. Sexes are alike.

Voice

Its song is a hollow cooing of 5 or so notes, usually repeated at least 3 times.

Feeding preferences

The Wood Pigeon has a varied diet of seeds and grain, leaves, fruits, berries, nuts, worms and insects.

Bird-table seed appeals to this heavyweight.

Nesting habits

Lays 1-2 eggs per clutch, and has 3 or more broods per year. The nest is a flimsy platform of sticks – you can often see the eggs when looking from below!

Look out for...

Adult Wood Pigeons feeding their young. Uniquely among British birds, they feed their offspring on a type of milk made in their crops.

Did you know?

The Wood Pigeon has a protracted breeding season. Individuals have been found sitting on eggs in every month of the year in Britain.

FERAL PIGEON

Identification
Comes in a bewildering variety of patterns and colours, including white, grey, brown and black – and often a mixture of them all! Many show a white rump and black wing bars. Often found in flocks. Sexes are alike.

Voice
Typical cooing calls that become very animated during the breeding season.

Feeding preferences
Feral Pigeons are used to scavenging for any kind of food they can find in towns and cities.

Nesting habits
Most nest on old buildings and under bridges, building a scant nest of twigs and all kinds of debris they find. Lays 1-2 eggs per clutch – at least 2 broods per year.

Did you know?
This is the domesticated version of the wild Rock Dove that nests on steep sea cliffs in the north and west of Britain.

Feral Pigeons are also called 'Town Pigeons' and can be very common in some cities.

PIED WAGTAIL

Identification

A well-named bird! This slender bird constantly wags its tail, and is boldly marked with black and white. Walks and runs on the ground and may be seen on larger, well-kept lawns, paths and rooftops, where there are plenty of insects to catch. The male (pictured) is more black and white and more crisply-marked than the female.

Voice

The call is distinctive once learned –'chi-sic'. The song is an extended version of the call.

Feeding preferences

Insects.

Nesting habits

The Pied Wagtail builds a nest of grass, moss, leaves, twigs and roots among piles of stone, in walls, banks and holes in buildings.

It lays 5-6 eggs per clutch and has 2-3 broods. The Pied Wagtail will use open-fronted nest-boxes

Look out for...

A Pied Wagtail interrupting its strut along the ground to pirouette upwards and catch a fly in its beak.

HOUSE MARTIN

Identification

A small, swallow-like bird that can be seen flying high over gardens, catching insects. Unlikely to be seen with its feet on land, apart from when visiting the nest or collecting nesting material.

The underparts are white, the cap is black, and the wings are black, glossed with blue. From above, a square white rump patch can be seen in front of the shallowly-forked black tail. Sexes are alike. The House Martin has a fluttery flight, with glides, twists and turns. They are usually found in flocks.

Voice

A quiet 'prit' flight call, and some buzzing song phrases.

Feeding preferences

Insects taken on the wing – mainly flies and aphids.

Nesting habits

Pairs build an unmistakable half cup nest from mud, under the eaves of houses, often in colonies. They will use artificial nests if they are provided.

The House Martin lays 4-5 white eggs per clutch – 2, occasionally 3, broods.

Look out for...

House Martins gathering wet mud from puddles in their beaks in late spring, and using it, painstakingly, to construct their nests.

SPARROWHAWK

Identification

Males are blue-grey above with attractive orange barring below. Females are larger, browner above and have black barring below. Both have piercing golden eyes, yellow legs and feet, and a short, hooked beak. Sparrowhawks fly with quick, clipped wingbeats interspersed with long glides on round wings.

Voice

Usually silent – a rarely heard, piercing 'kek, kek, kek'.

Feeding preferences

Feeds mainly on small birds, with a few mammals, insects and amphibians.

Nesting habits

Stick and twig nest, usually built in a tree. Lays 3-4 blue or white eggs per clutch. Single-brooded.

Look out for...

'Skydiving' display flights in spring in which the pair rise high up into the air and fly around with curious 'elastic' wingbeats, before plummeting back down to earth with wings closed.

Did you know?

The Sparrowhawk suffered a drastic decline in the 1950s and 60s because of the use of toxic agricultural chemicals. This seriously affected the breeding success of birds of prey because they laid eggs with shells that were too thin. The Sparrowhawk has only recently recovered its numbers and returned to its natural range.

SWIFT

Identification
Like a black boomerang in shape because of its long, scythe shaped wings, small head and tail. The plumage is black, apart from a paler throat.

The Swift spends long periods gliding around and then shooting across the sky with rapid wingbeats. A gregarious bird. Sexes are alike.

Voice
High-pitched screaming cries, and a harsh trill.

Feeding preferences
Insects taken solely on the wing.

Nesting habits
Often nests in colonies, in crevices, thatch, under house eaves or rock faces. Lays 2-3 white eggs in the nest of straw, grass and feathers. It will use special artificial Swift boxes. Single-brooded.

Look out for...
Parties of Swifts engaged in their pre-nuptials, chasing through the streets at head height, making a real din with their screaming calls.

Did you know?
The Swift only comes to land to rear its young. It mates, and even sleeps, on the wing!

Other birds that may visit your garden occasionally include: Mallard, MarshTit, Treecreeper, Kingfisher, GreyWagtail, Grey Heron, Reed Bunting, Linnet, Lesser Redpoll, Swallow, Waxwing, Pheasant, Tawny Owl and Carrion Crow.

THE GARDEN BIRD YEAR

W ild birds have an active lifestyle, which often changes week by week as the seasons progress, providing the garden bird-watcher with entertainment throughout the year.

WINTER (December–February)

Winters in Britain are getting milder, but this is still a tough time for birds. Natural food is scarce and birds spend the vast majority of the much-reduced daylight hours feeding in order to survive. Many small birds have to eat 30 per cent of their body weight on a daily basis to survive in cold weather.

Keep the garden well stocked with food, and it is certain to be packed with birds every day.

Winter visitors

The number of birds and the variety of species in your garden will probably be at its highest at this time, and cold snaps can result in unusual visitors to the garden as well as bringing in larger numbers of the more regular birds. Many birds leave the countryside to seek shelter, as well as food, in warmer, built-up areas.

You may attract a wintering Chiffchaff or Blackcap with bird-table offerings, and urban gardens may be visited by species more usually associated with the countryside, such as Reed Buntings or Bramblings. Redwings arrive without fail in my garden soon after the first hard overnight frosts of winter, and they join the resident Blackbirds and Song

Starlings can be seen going to roost in the late afternoon.

Robins provide a constant cabaret in winter as they defend their territories.

Thrushes feeding on berry-laden shrubs, such as pyracantha and holly.

Mistle Thrushes jealously guard their favourite berry bush at this time – they certainly don't like to share! They may defend a single bush for several weeks, only taking berries that are necessary – unlike some thrushes, which will strip a bush in a matter of days.

Another species that vigorously defends its winter territory is the Robin. Males and females hold separate territories at this time, and watching Robins in winter will always provide entertainment. Few birds sing in winter and it can be very quiet in terms of bird sound. However, you can still hear Robins singing to protect the boundaries of their winter territories.

One bird that every keen garden watcher should hope for in winter is the Waxwing. This beautiful, crested bird, named after the red and yellow tips to its wing feathers that look like hot wax, is a winter visitor from Scandinavia.

Large numbers may arrive if the berry crop is poor or exhausted on the Continent – then you may well receive a visit from a party of these unmistakable and very exciting wanderers. This is yet another reason for planting a few berry-bearing shrubs.

You may see large flocks of Starlings heading to their communal roosts over the garden, late in the afternoon. They may roost nearby if there are large trees. They make a spectacular sight, twisting and turning like a giant cloud of smoke in the sky.

THE GARDEN BIRD YEAR

In spring, courtship becomes a top priority.

SPRING
(March-May)

The first signs of spring, as the days start to lengthen, are extremely welcome and there is no more soul-lifting sound than that of birdsong. The intensity and variety of song in spring (especially May, when the dawn chorus is at its very best) is incredible.

Many birds start to tune up early in the season with 'sub-song'. This is a warm-up for the main performance and sounds quieter, shorter and a bit half-hearted. It really does sound as if the birds are practising to get their voices into top condition.

You can sense the excitement among garden birds at this time of year, and their activities will provide endless hours of pleasure.

Spring activity

One of the first garden birds to burst into song is the Mistle Thrush, which can be in full song in March. Its wild, far-carrying song, uttered from a prominent perch, is a sure sign of the change of season.

The 'squeaky bicycle-wheel' song of the Great Tit is another sign that spring is on its way, and pairs of this colourful garden resident start to engage in animated, high-speed chases around the garden.

Territorial disputes between rival birds are commonplace as boundaries are made, and claims are staked for nesting sites as the birds' thoughts switch from survival to reproduction.

Courtship

Many garden birds display to accompany their songs. The Collared Dove rises up into the air from a favourite perch, and with cooing calls, claps its wings at the peak and glides elegantly back down to earth with its wings stretched out. This is great to watch, as is the bat-like display of Greenfinches overhead and the comical 'wing-shaking' song display of the Starling.

It is vital for birds to get into peak condition ready for the rigours of the breeding season. It takes an enormous amount of energy to produce and lay a clutch of eggs, and clutch size and the number of broods attempted, often depends on how much food is available and how fit the females are.

Although the needs of their young are paramount, adult birds also have to make sure they keep themselves in top condition so that they can care for their young, finding and delivering the large amount of food they need.

Nesting

A sure sign that birds are thinking of breeding in, or near, your garden is the sight of birds gathering nesting material and investigating potential nest sites – perhaps including any nest-boxes you may have erected. In some species, it is the male that presents potential nest sites to his mate for the final once over! It is vital to choose a suitable, safe site – and much time goes into the selection process. Some species build several nests.

The sudden disappearance of female birds is a sure sign that they are on nests and eggs, and the first signs of breeding success are adult birds collecting food in their beaks to take back to their nests. The proud parents will be grateful for some food while they are gathering goodies for their demanding brood, so keep providing it for them.

March and April can be very variable months in terms of temperature, and strong winds and rain are frequent. Prolonged bad weather can be disastrous for early-nesting resident birds, such as Blackbirds, Song Thrushes, Robins and Collared Doves, as eggs and young chill very easily, and parents may be unable to find enough food.

Migrants

Spring is also an exciting time because the resident garden birds are joined by species that spent the winter thousands of miles away in Africa. Amazingly, it is highly likely that the pair of Swifts or House Martins you see are the same ones that spent the previous summer feeding on insects over your garden, or raising broods of young under the eaves or on the rafters of your house, garage or shed.

Swifts are one of the last migrant birds to return from Africa, and it may be well into May before they arrive, coinciding with the time when large numbers of flying insects are on the wing. It is incredible how the birds seem to know and get their timing just right!

THE GARDEN BIRD YEAR

SUMMER
(June–August)

The appearance of young birds in the garden is an exciting yet worrying time as the helpless-looking youngsters flutter around. They may look extremely vulnerable, but you can be sure their parents are not far away.

Rearing young

In some cases, as with Blackbirds, the male looks after the young while the female gets to work on the next brood. Birds that raise only one brood, such as Blue Tits, roam around the garden in family parties, searching for insects. Tits time the hatching of their nestlings to coincide with the appearance of caterpillars.

Families of birds stay together after the young have left the nest, and the young continue to be fed by the parents. The 'begging' posture of baby birds looks very comical. With wings quivering and wide gapes, they call to their parents for food.

Eventually, young birds will become independent and start to wander further afield. Once they are fully grown and can feed themselves, they will leave the sanctuary of the garden.

TOP TIP

Make a muddy puddle in an open area and keep it wet for House Martins. Their nests sometimes fall apart because of a shortage of wet mud.

Birds, such as these Swallows, are kept fully occupied when they have chicks in the nest.

The male Blackbird will take care of the first brood while the female is hatching the second.

Summer moult

Adult birds can look very ragged and bedraggled after the rigours of raising a family. They will need to moult and replace their feathers ready for winter. Some species may go to ground for a few weeks while they grow their new feathers, so 'familiar friends' may go missing for a bit. Birds are at their most vulnerable during times of moult, so they need to keep well out of sight. It takes a lot of energy to complete a moult.

Juveniles

Many juvenile birds can be recognised because of their large gape patches around their beak. They are also very fresh and neat-looking because of the brand new feathers they are boasting.

Starlings start to flock on the lawn and in the streets, and the brown juveniles really stand out among the black adults. They bicker among themselves and fight over scraps.

Departees

Flocks of House Martins and Swifts grow during the summer as the young birds join the adults. They will have to depart for Africa soon. Most Swifts leave the country during August, and the skies may seem strangely quiet without their calls. House Martins stay a little later, but town breeders may depart for insect-packed lakes and reedbeds to make sure they are fully fed for their long journey.

The sky above the garden will seem quiet and empty, but the aerial acrobats will return next spring.

DID YOU KNOW?

Birds like to sunbathe in the garden as much as we do. Blackbirds do this regularly. They lie almost flat and hold out their wings and tail to absorb ultra-violet light.

THE GARDEN BIRD YEAR

The Great Tit, and other members of the tit family, may leave your garden during the autumn months.

AUTUMN (September–November)

For many bird gardeners, this is the quietest time of year, and it is not uncommon for the number of birds visiting gardens to decrease. The abundance of natural food in the countryside at this time means that many birds spend much of their time taking advantage of the natural bounty on offer.

Preparing for winter

Hedgerows are full of berries, and, before the first frosts come, there are still plenty of insects to eat.

Considerate farmers will have left autumn stubble, and the fields are full of the spilt grain. Many wildflowers are setting seed and these also provide plenty of natural food for birds.

Tit families may leave the garden and join up with other families from the surrounding area to form 'post-breeding' flocks that roam the countryside. The same applies to other communal species, such as finches, House Sparrows and Starlings.

So don't be concerned if you find that fewer birds are visiting your garden at this time. They are just having a bit of a holiday and will be back when winter starts to take hold. Young birds start to look more adult-like after their post-juvenile moult, when they replace some of their juvenile feathers with the adult versions. Don't be concerned if 'your' babies seem to have vanished – they have just grown up!

Comings and goings

Listen on still, starry nights for the piercing, lisping call of Redwings. These attractive thrushes migrate at night, using the stars to help them make their way south from Iceland and Scandinavia. At night, you can hear the contact calls of flocks passing over the garden from late September until the end of the year.

If you look up during autumn mornings, you may spot incoming birds such as Fieldfares and Redwings. The flocks of Starlings that are flying high over the garden in the morning may well be some of the many Russian immigrants that join our own birds for the long, cold winter ahead.

The Fieldfare will reach the UK in the autumn.

79

USEFUL CONTACTS

Here are the contact details of wild bird organisations with a particular interest and knowledge of garden birds and suppliers of equipment and bird food. The RSPB and BTO organise garden bird recording events, such as 'The Big Garden Birdwatch', on a regular basis, which you can take part in and help contribute to our knowledge of wild birds, their behaviour and population trends.

The Royal Society for the Protection of Birds (RSPB)
For general information and advice on wild birds and retailer of its own range of bird foods and other garden bird products.

RSPB, The Lodge, Sandy, Bedfordshire SG19 2DL.
Tel: 01767 680551.
www.rspb.org.uk

British Trust for Ornithology
For general information on wild birds and relevant scientific studies.

BTO, The Nunnery, Thetford, Norfolk IP24 2PU.
Tel: 01842 750050.
info@bto.org
www.bto.org

Gardman
Garden product and bird care specialists.

Gardman Ltd, High Street, Moulton, Spalding, Lincolnshire PE12 6QD.
Tel: 01406 372227.
customerservices@gardman.co.uk
www.gardman.co.uk

CJ Wildbird Foods
Wild bird food and equipment suppliers.

CJ Wildbird Foods Ltd, The Rea, Upton Magna, Shrewsbury SY4 4UR.
Tel: 0800 731 2820.
advice@birdfood.co.uk
www.birdfood.co.uk/dev/

Haiths
Wild bird food and equipment suppliers.

J E Haith Ltd, 65 Park Street, Cleethorpes, North East Lincolnshire DN35 7NF.
Tel: 0800 298 7054.
enquiries@haiths.com
www.haiths.com

Starlings going to roost in the early evening.